D1325460

RED MIST

FOOTBALL'S MOST SHOCKING MOMENTS

RED CARDS, DIRTY TACKLES, HEADBUTTS, PITCH INVADERS AND MORE

Hardie Grant

BOOKS

RED MIST

FOOTBALL'S MOST SHOCKING MOMENTS

RED CARDS, DIRTY TACKLES, HEADBUTTS, PITCH INVADERS AND MORE

by Phil Cartwright

Illustrated by Chester Holme

CONTENTS

Where the moment
took place

When the moment
took place

When the moment
resulted in a red card

YELLOW CARDS DIRTY TACKLES HEADBUTTS BRAWLS PUNCHING KUNG-FU KICKS AND FLYING BOOTS

RED
CARDS
DIRTY
CHEATS
HANDBAGS
BITES
SLAPPING
BALL
GRABBING
AND A
FLYING
HAIRDRYER

Let me take you back to the 2006 World Cup final between Italy and France. What's the first thing that springs to mind when you think of that game? Probably not the match itself. It wasn't a classic. Nor is it likely to be David Trezeguet's penalty shootout miss that resulted in Italy becoming world champions for a fourth time.

No. What everyone undoubtedly remembers from the 2006 final is France captain, Zinedine Zidane, signing off on a most exceptional career by headbutting Italian defender, Marco Materazzi, in the chest (see page 16). That red card remains one of the most talked-about moments in sporting history, and also one of the most misunderstood. Just what caused Zidane, one of the most gifted footballers ever, to completely lose it on the grandest stage in football?

The truth is that the old red mist is never too far away in football – whatever level you're watching, playing, or managing at. It doesn't matter whether it's at five-a-side with your mates, or in an international tournament watched by billions – anger, revenge, frustration, or downright stupidity can appear in a split-second.

NTRO

And often there's no explanation for it. These emotions pop up in the heat of the moment, but that can lead to disastrous consequences for everyone concerned. No player, manager, or even team is infallible. Even the coolest characters in the world can sometimes burn white-hot at the most inopportune times.

Red Mist: Football's Most Shocking Moments takes a look back at some of the most despicable incidents, when the pressures of local rivalry, league status, or national pride simply got too much for those involved. Revisited and illustrated in this book are bad tackles, headbutts, bites, fights between teammates, and many more jaw-dropping moments when the beautiful game showed its ugly side.

**Red Mist *(noun, informal)*
A feeling of extreme competitiveness or anger that temporarily clouds one's judgment.**

THE OXFORD DICTIONARY OF
ENGLISH, DEFINITION

THE RULES FOR YELLOW AND RED CARDS

Like any sport, football has strict rules and guidelines. If you break them, you must prepare to face the consequences.

FIFA, football's governing body, produces a *Laws of the Game* document each season.

The difference between success and failure, especially at an elite level, is so vast that players will often try to bend the rules to their advantage as much as they can to gain an edge – but sometimes they overstep the mark.

Referees are permitted to take disciplinary action against anyone who goes outside those rules. They can show either a **yellow card** (a lesser sanction, which is essentially a caution for a player) or a **red card** (a more serious punishment, for which players will be sent from the field and not be allowed to take any further part in the match).

——> Visit www.fifa.com/development/education-and-technical/referees/laws-of-the-game.html for more information

—→ YELLOW CARD

There are several indiscretions for which a player, substitute or substituted player (you don't have to be on the pitch to be disciplined) can be shown a yellow card:

—— Persistent fouling is probably the most common bookable offence. Players usually get away with the odd trip of an opponent here and a mistimed challenge there, but one offence too many and the referee will show that player a yellow card.

—— Several offences come under the banner of "unsporting behaviour", including: attempting to deceive the officials by feigning injury or diving in a bid to earn a free-kick or penalty, a reckless (but not dangerous) tackle that results in a foul, or handling the ball in an attempt to score a goal.

—— Goal celebrations deemed as "excessive" can also result in a yellow card. If a player removes his shirt when celebrating a goal, that is an automatic yellow-card offence. So, too, is approaching the crowd in a manner that could cause safety or security issues.

—— Time-wasting or delaying play is also considered to be an offence worthy of a caution. As with persistent fouling, it is something that a referee will usually verbally warn a player about, before then issuing a yellow card if it continues to happen during the match.

⟶ RED CARD

More serious offences are punished with a red card. A player will be sent off if they are guilty of two yellow-card offences, but will be immedietely sent from the field if they do any of the following:

—— Any act of violent conduct, including kicks, punches and headbutts. Whether the player in question makes contact with their intended target is irrelevant; if they use excessive force against an opponent or official when not competing for the ball, they should be punished with a red card.

—— Endanger an opponent during play. This ruling takes in two-footed tackles and forceful challenges that put an opponent's safety at risk

—— Deny a clear opportunity for a goal. An outfield player who handles the ball to prevent it crossing the goal line should be sent off. That sanction also applies to players who commit a foul on a player who has a genuine chance to score. However, there are occasions when a yellow card will be shown instead, if the referee deems that the guilty player made an honest attempt to play the ball.

—— Bite or spit at an opponent, or use abusive language or gestures.

PLAYERS

When players take to the pitch, they – and only they – are responsible for their actions. Once there, anything can, and often does, happen.

ZIDANE'S HEADBUTT

OLYMPIASTADION,
BERLIN, GERMANY

9 JULY
2006

It is difficult to think of any player whose career ended in a more ignominious way than Zinedine Zidane. The 2006 World Cup final could, and perhaps should, have been the fairytale ending for the most talented footballer of his generation. Instead, it turned into a nightmare for France's captain. Eight years earlier, Zidane had become the darling of French football by leading his country to World Cup glory on home soil. His two headed goals in France's 3-0 win over Brazil instantly lifted him to iconic status, in a team that became a political symbol of how the different parts of France's multicultural society could come together for good.

French football had its ups and downs in the years that followed. Zidane starred for a victorious France at Euro 2000, but *Les Bleus* made an abysmal defence of the World Cup in 2002 and Zidane retired from international football after a quarter-final exit to Greece at Euro 2004. With France struggling to qualify for the 2006 World Cup, Zidane was persuaded to end his international exile in the summer of 2005, eventually leading his country to top spot in their group. Zidane signalled his intention to retire at the end of the tournament in Germany, and what better way to bow out than by winning a second World Cup?

Zidane was an inspiration during the tournament. His performances were outstanding on the way to his swansong in Berlin, which contributed him being voted the best player in the competition.

A rugged, defensive Italian side lay in wait but Zidane's final match started perfectly: France were awarded an early penalty and Zidane coolly chipped the ball past Gianluigi Buffon to put his side in front. Marco Materazzi equalised, and the final went to extra-time, when the controversial incident occurred.

> **"I was tugging his shirt, he said to me 'if you want my shirt so much I'll give it to you afterwards,' I answered that I'd prefer his sister ..."**
>
> MARCO MATERAZZI

During a stoppage in play, Zidane was walking away from Materazzi when he turned sharply and headbutted the Italian centre-back in the chest.

What exactly happened to cause such a reaction? In an interview with *Gazzetta dello Sport* a couple of months after the confrontation, Materazzi said: "I was tugging his shirt, he said to me 'if you want my shirt so much I'll give it to you afterwards,' I answered that I'd prefer his sister. It's not a particularly nice thing to say, I recognise that. But loads of players say worse things. I didn't even know he had a sister before all this happened."

The incident had not been shown live, and broadcasters struggled to understand what was happening as events unfolded on the pitch. There was a sense of disbelief as Zidane was shown a red card and, in what became an iconic image of the incident, he walked off the field without even as much as a glance at the World Cup trophy gleaming brightly by the side of the pitch. Replays helped the millions watching worldwide to see what had caused the dismissal.

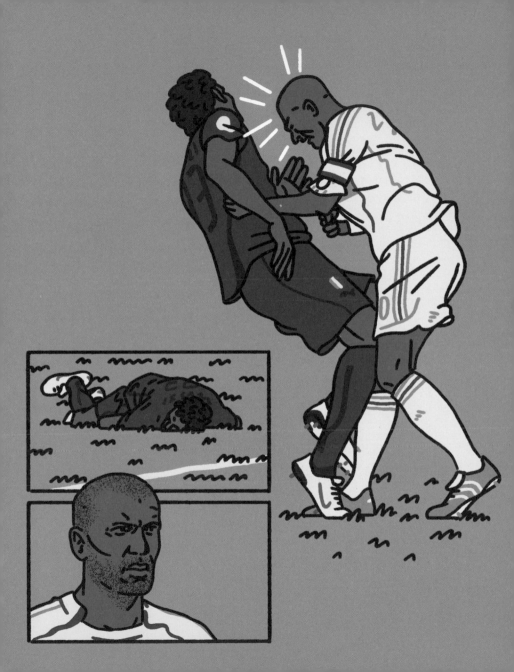

Italy emerged as world champions after the game went to a penalty shootout. Would France have won that World Cup if Zidane had stayed on? It is a question that can never be answered. The French press showed their disappointment with a series of critical headlines the following day, but the general mood among the French people was a supportive one. Thousands chanted Zidane's name at the team's homecoming, while President Jacques Chirac said the country was "extremely proud" of its captain. Six years later, a statue of Zidane's headbutt on Materazzi was unveiled in Paris, demonstrating that Zidane's epic red-mist moment of madness had transcended the sport and made a wider cultural impact. •

"You can't excuse that. Zidane's career ends in disgrace."

BBC COMMENTATOR, JOHN MOTSON

ERIC CANTONA'S

SELHURST PARK, LONDON, U.K.

25 JANUARY 1995

KUNG-FU KICK

ENIGMATIC, ELEGANT, EXTRAORDINARY

Eric Cantona was one of the biggest stars of the Premier League's formative years. The Frenchman was renowned for his brilliant skills and was a scorer of simply breathtaking goals. Manchester United fans fondly remember him as "King Eric". But there was a dark side, too.

He was shown three red cards while playing for United during the 1993–94 season, including two in consecutive matches that resulted in a five-match ban. The moment that really stunned English football came in January 1995. In a league game away at Crystal Palace, Cantona was dismissed early in the second half for kicking out at Palace defender Richard Shaw. As he made his way down the touchline towards the tunnel, Cantona explosively reacted to abusive comments from a Palace supporter. Without warning, the Frenchman leapt feet-first over the advertising hoardings and kicked the supporter, kung-fu style, in the stomach. Cantona followed his audacious lunge up with a flurry of punches, before being pulled away.

The recriminations were severe. United fined him £20,000 and suspended him for four months – a sanction that was enough to rule him out of the remainder of the season. The Football Association (FA) went further still, extending the ban to eight months and increasing the fine by another £10,000. Many who saw the incident on TV or followed the story in the papers felt he should have been thrown out of the game for good.

There were also criminal charges. Cantona pleaded guilty to common assault and was sentenced to two weeks in prison, although his punishment was reduced on appeal to 120 hours of community service.

At a media press conference afterwards, Cantona delivered an enigmatic 17-word statement that became as famous as the incident itself: "When the seagulls follow the trawler, it's because they think sardines will be thrown into the sea." Many have interpreted this to be a veiled statement about the media: they are the seagulls following Cantona's metaphorical trawler, feeding on any scrap of information on the incident that he might part with.

As his ban dragged on, an increasingly-frustrated Cantona nearly left England. The club managed to convince him to stay at Old Trafford and he again became a pivotal figure for United once his ban had been completed. Typically, he scored in his first game back and would lead the club to a domestic double in 1995–96, netting a sublime winning goal in their FA Cup final victory over Liverpool at Wembley. Cantona played one more season at United before retiring unexpectedly at the young age of 30 in 1997. •

"When the seagulls follow the trawler, it's because they think sardines will be thrown into the sea."

ERIC CANTONA

SCHU-MACHER

ESTADIO RAMÓN SÁNCHEZ PIZJUÁN, SEVILLE, SPAIN

**8 JULY
1982**

BATTERS BATTISTON

Mention the names of either French defender Patrick Battiston or German goalkeeper Toni Schumacher, and one incident will spring immediately to mind. It was the 1982 World Cup semi-final between France and West Germany in Seville. It is remembered as one of the best games in World Cup history, but also for a collision between the two protagonists that left Battiston with damaged vertebrae, cracked ribs, and two teeth missing.

Battiston had just been brought on as a second-half substitute when his forward run was picked out by a sumptuous through-ball from Michel Platini. Platini's pass had sliced the German defence in two, causing Schumacher to race off his line. Battiston got a foot on the ball, but his shot rolled just wide of the post. Schumacher, meanwhile, had jumped into the air, and his momentum caused his hips and legs to crash into Battiston, crumpling the Frenchman. The severity of Battiston's injuries quickly became clear, but there was no card given against Schumacher. In fact, France weren't even awarded a free-kick! While an unconscious Battiston was being carried off on a stretcher, Schumacher stood impassively waiting to restart play.

"Secretly, I feared Battiston was seriously injured, possibly lying in a coma."

TONI SCHUMACHER

That reaction, as well as Schumacher's role in the collision, drew huge criticism. A careless comment in his post-match interview did not help either. When informed that Battiston had lost teeth, Schumacher said he would pay for his dental bills. Schumacher made a public apology to Battiston a few days later and has since said there are plenty of things he regrets about the incident: not checking on Battiston's condition was one, with the anger of the French players surrounding their team-mate given as one of the reasons for keeping his distance in the immediate aftermath.

He told French newspaper *Le Figaro* in 2012: "I regret that the German delegation and myself didn't go to the hospital to get the news about Patrick Battiston. Secretly, I feared Battiston was seriously injured, possibly lying in a coma." Thankfully, Battiston made a full recovery, and was part of the France team that became European champions two years later. •

KEANE EVENS THE SCORE

**OLD TRAFFORD,
MANCHESTER, U.K.**

**21 APRIL
2001**

WITH
HAALAND

Premier League statistics at the start of the 2018–19 season showed that only three players have received more red cards than Roy Keane. One of the driving forces of Manchester United's dominance of English football during the 1990s and beyond, Keane's insatiable will to win often got him into trouble. He was dismissed seven times in the Premier League, but what made his red card in a local derby against Manchester City in 2001 a little bit different were the revelations afterwards, and the row that rumbled on for more than a decade later.

The story begins in 1997 when "Alfie" Haaland, playing for Leeds United, and Keane collided. Though it looked innocuous, Keane suffered a damaged cruciate ligament, which kept him out of action for almost a year. Convinced that the United captain was feigning his injury, Haaland berated a prostrate Keane. It was a moment the Republic of Ireland midfielder wouldn't forget in a hurry.

"I've kicked lots of players and I know the difference between hurting somebody and injuring somebody. I didn't go to injure Haaland."

ROY KEANE

Fast forward to 2001, with Haaland now playing for United's local rivals Manchester City. As both players went in for a 50-50 challenge, Keane raised his studs and crashed into the side of Haaland's right knee, sending Haaland sprawling. Keane was shown an immediate red card, but before he left the pitch, he stood over and shouted at his prone foe, repaying the favour Haaland had showed him four years earlier. Though Keane received a three-match ban and £5,000 fine, the incident proved to have an epilogue.

Keane's first autobiography, published in 2002, suggested that he had deliberately attempted to injure Haaland. Keane protested that his comments were misconstrued by his ghost writer using "artistic licence," but he was banned for five games and fined at a Football Association disciplinary hearing as a result. In a second book, published in 2014, Keane said there was "no premeditation" and there was "no wish to injure" Haaland, but in the end, did concede, admitting that he wanted to "hurt" the Norwegian. Haaland would never play a full game of football again, and retired in 2003. There is debate over how much Keane was to blame for that, however, as Haaland had long been battling injuries to his left knee, the one Keane didn't connect with. •

ALVARADO
NEUTRALISES

AMSTERDAM ARENA,
AMSTERDAM, THE NETHERLANDS

21 DECEMBER
2011

PITCH
INVADER

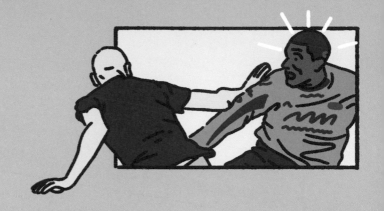

Fans are a crucial part of any football match; at the end of the day, what is sport without people going to watch it? Sometimes the "12th player" can seem to be the difference between victory and defeat, but at other times, a fan's passion can boil over in all kinds of terrible ways.

In 2011, a Dutch Cup tie between Ajax and AZ Alkmaar was abandoned after Alkmaar goalkeeper, Esteban Alvarado, was accosted by an Ajax supporter who had invaded the pitch. Alvarado was standing on the edge of his penalty area as his team made progress further up the pitch. Unbeknownst to him, a drunk spectator had broken free of a steward and was racing towards him. Alvarado saw him at the last second, and managed to aim a flying kick at his would-be attacker, flooring the Ajax fan. The Costa Rican preceded to kick the pitch invader twice in retaliation – but was surprised when referee, Bas Nijhuis, sent him off for misconduct as a result.

Alvarado and his team-mates were furious with the decision. AZ's manager, Gertjan Verbeek, ordered his players to leave the field and the last-16 match was called off with Ajax leading 1-0.

Alvarado's red card was later rescinded, and the teenage pitch invader was given a prison sentence, and banned from Ajax games for life. The replayed match took place behind closed doors and Alkmaar won it 3-2, progressing to the semi-finals before losing to Heracles. •

"I understand that Esteban was defending himself, but he walked to him and kicked him multiple times. He could also have walked away."

REFEREE, BAS NIJHUIS

BECKHAM LASHES OUT

**STADE GEOFFREY GUICHARD,
SAINT-ÉTIENNE, FRANCE**

**30 JUNE
1998**

AT SIMEONE

David Beckham had the world at his feet in the summer of 1998. Off the field, he was a style icon, one of Britain's most marketable sportsmen and engaged to a world-famous pop star. On the field, he was an integral part of a Manchester United team that had dominated English club football for much of the decade. He could do no wrong. Or could he? Left out of the team for England's first two World Cup group matches, the clamour for Beckham's inclusion in the starting line-up grew. He justified his selection against Colombia with a wonderful free-kick to help England through to the last 16, where Argentina awaited in Saint-Étienne.

Shortly after half-time, with the match level at 2-2, Beckham shaped to receive a pass on the halfway line. Argentina midfielder Diego Simeone crashed into the back of England's number seven, sending him sprawling to the floor. As Simeone bent down to apologise, Beckham flicked out his right foot and down went Simeone. There was little force behind the kick – it was essentially a tap on the back of Simeone's calf. Certainly not enough to injure, but enough to trip Simeone and send him falling to the ground. It all happened right in front of the referee, who found himself surrounded by Argentina's players demanding Beckham be ejected from the game.

Simeone has since admitted that he "took advantage" of Beckham's petulance to try to get him sent off. And it worked: Beckham received a straight red card for the kick. England battled gamely with 10 men and took the match to a penalty shootout, which they lost. With England out of the World Cup, Beckham was instantly cast as the villain, many believing his momentary lapse of discipline had cost his country dearly.

He was pilloried by the press and castigated by opposition supporters. There was even an effigy of Beckham seen hanging outside a London pub. This was a level of abuse that no English footballer had ever experienced before, nor since. Beckham apologised for his actions, and set about helping Manchester United win the treble in 1999. By the end of 2000, he was England captain.

For all of his club success, it was four years after his dismissal against Argentina that he finally achieved true redemption. Having almost single-handedly led his country to the 2002 World Cup with an all-action display in a qualifier against Greece, Beckham netted the winner from the penalty spot in a World Cup group match against ... you guessed it: Argentina. •

"As I was trying to stand up that was when he kicked me from behind, and I took advantage of that. I think any person would have taken advantage of that in just the same way."

DIEGO SIMEONE

RIJKAARD SPITS AT VÖLLER

SAN SIRO, MILAN, ITALY

24 JUNE 1990

One of the most unsavoury moments of the 1990 World Cup came when West Germany met the Netherlands. The two nations' rivalry is one of the fiercest in international football (originating in the German invasion and occupation of the Netherlands during World War II), and it came to the fore again during their second-round meeting in Milan. West Germany won the match 2-1 to reach the last eight and would eventually lift the trophy, but their victory over the Dutch is most remembered for an ugly incident between Netherlands' Frank Rijkaard and German striker Rudi Völler.

Völler was brought down midway inside the Dutch half by Rijkaard, who was cautioned. Enraged by his punishment – which meant that he would now miss the quarter-final should Holland progress – Rijkaard spat in Völler's carefully coiffed mullet as he ran back to his position. Understandably furious, Völler confronted Rijkaard, but also ended up getting booked by the referee, who was seemingly uninterested in his protestations.

From the resulting free-kick, Völler went in for a challenge with the Netherlands goalkeeper, Hans van Breukelen, and fell to

the ground, despite making minimal contact, if any. Another confrontation ensued, with Rijkaard standing over the grounded Völler, attempting to drag him up by the ear. Once Völler got up, Rijkaard stamped on his foot, causing him to fall to the ground, once more.

Both players were promptly sent off by the referee, and as Völler stood pondering his dismissal, Rijkaard ran past and spat at him for a second time. Rijkaard – who went on to manage his national team and Barcelona – apologised for his actions, and the duo buried the hatchet by appearing in a television commercial together some years later. For many, though, the hostility between two of the world's greatest international teams was never as clear as during these few minutes, when even basic human decency went out the window. •

"There was no doubt about it then ... Rijkaard spat on Völler as he walked past him, and that is atrocious."

BBC COMMENTATOR, TONY GUBBA

DI CANIO

**HILLSBOROUGH STADIUM,
SHEFFIELD, U.K.**

**26 SEPTEMBER
1998**

VS.
REFEREE

Paolo Di Canio had the ability to do some incredible things on a football field that would take your breath away.

There was the sublime: sensational scissor-kicks, silky skills and, at times, great sportsmanship. While playing for West Ham United, Di Canio passed up the chance to score a late winner into an almost-empty net at Goodison Park, catching a cross when he saw Everton goalkeeper Paul Gerrard was lying injured near the corner flag – an act that earned Di Canio a FIFA Fair Play award. And then there was the ridiculous. In September 1998, Di Canio was given one of the longest bans in English history – 11 matches – for shoving referee Paul Alcock over while playing for Sheffield Wednesday.

It all started fairly innocently. Arsenal midfielder Patrick Vieira reacted to his shirt being pulled by Wednesday's Wim Jonk by pushing the Dutchman to the ground. A melee of players, including Di Canio, quickly assembled to push and shove each other. It rapidly escalated, however, and Di Canio aimed a kick at the leg of Arsenal defender Martin Keown. The Italian was marshalled away from trouble by some of his Wednesday teammates, but Alcock had already seen enough of a transgression to warrant a dismissal.

Di Canio's reaction to seeing Alcock brandish a red card was to push him hard in the chest, causing Alcock to fall backwards to the ground. There was a comical element to Alcock's seemingly never-ending fall, as there was when Gunners full-back, Nigel Winterburn, attempted to confront Di Canio as he left the field, but then recoiled quickly when it appeared Di Canio was about to square up to him. The absurdity of the incident didn't take away from the general sense of shock surrounding it, and the furore that followed afterwards.

Di Canio was banned for 11 games and fined £10,000. He never played for Sheffield Wednesday again, joining West Ham a few months later, where he became a club legend. •

"Paolo's reacted and I can't condone it. It's absolute stupidity and I don't know what's gone through his mind."

SHEFFIELD WEDNESDAY MANAGER, DANNY WILSON

SUÁREZ

VARIOUS STADIUMS

BITES

REPEAT OFFENCES

BACK

Luis Suárez is one of those footballers in the modern era that you absolutely love if he's on your team, and love to hate if he's playing for somebody else. Suárez scored for fun at Ajax, Liverpool and Barcelona. He is also Uruguay's record scorer, with 53 goals for his country by the end of the 2018 World Cup. Unfortunately, his unquestionable ability and his status as one of the best players in the world has often been clouded by his poor disciplinary record.

First up, there is the deliberate handball that denied Ghana a place in the 2010 World Cup semi-final. Suárez used his hand to prevent an almost-certain goal in the closing seconds of extra-time, and was sent off as a result. Most players would probably have done the same in his situation, however, it was his ecstatic celebration on the touchline, when Ghana's Asamoah Gyan failed to score the resulting spot-kick, that left a bitter taste. Uruguay were ultimately victorious in a penalty shootout, meaning Ghana missed out on becoming the first African nation to reach the last four of a World Cup.

Then, in 2011, Suárez denied claims that he had racially abused Manchester United defender Patrice Evra, but the Football Association found him guilty of the charge and he was suspended for eight games.

And lastly, there were the biting incidents. His first major brush with the authorities on this front came while he was with Dutch club Ajax in 2010. Suárez bit PSV Eindhoven midfielder Otman Bakkal on the shoulder and was banned for seven matches, earning him the nickname of "The Cannibal of Ajax" from a Dutch newspaper. He joined Liverpool a couple of months later, and would again be the subject of controversy at his new club. Suárez received a 10-match ban for biting Chelsea defender Branislav Ivanović on the elbow in 2013. The event was shocking enough for UK prime minister, David Cameron, to weigh in, suggesting that the English FA get tough on the Uruguayan.

However, his biggest sanction came following another biting incident at the 2014 World Cup. During Uruguay's final group match against Italy on 24th June, Suárez and Italian centre-back, Giorgio Chiellini, clashed off the ball, with Suárez choosing again to bite his opponent on the shoulder. The match officials did not see it, but FIFA retrospectively clamped down hard, imposing a four-month suspension. Suárez lost sponsorships, his World Cup was over, and he did not play for his new club, Barcelona, until late October.

While often drawing the ire of opposition supporters for sometimes going down too easily under challenges, Suárez appears to have adopted a much calmer approach in the latter part of his career. He keeps on scoring goals, he keeps on winning trophies, and he has more-or-less steered clear of making the headlines for the wrong reasons. •

"I apologise to Giorgio Chiellini and the entire football family. I vow to the public that there will never again be another incident like this."

LUIS SUÁREZ

DUNCAN DISORDE

IBROX STADIUM, GLASGOW, U.K.

16 APRIL 1994

HEADBUTT

RLY'S

Three players hold the unwanted record of the most red cards in Premier League history: Richard Dunne, Patrick Vieira, and Duncan Ferguson. The most famous of Ferguson's red-mist moments did not result in a red card, but made him the first British professional footballer to be jailed for an on-field offence.

The towering Scottish striker was just 21 when Glasgow Rangers paid a British record transfer fee of £4 million to sign him in 1993. Unfortunately, his year-long stay at Ibrox was marred by one incident in a match against Raith Rovers in 1994.

"I have spent an entire career trying to shake off a reputation I earned in one day."

DUNCAN FERGUSON

A tit-for-tat tussle near the corner flag ended with Ferguson headbutting Raith's defender Jock McStay. Referee Kenny Clark decided against showing Ferguson a card at the time, but Ferguson was later charged with – and convicted of – assault.

It wasn't Ferguson's first time falling foul of the law, and his previous convictions resulted in him being landed with a three-month jail sentence in October 1995, by which time he had joined English Premier League side Everton.

Ferguson spent 44 days in prison before resuming a career that showed flashes of his talent, but was too often punctured by injury problems and suspensions. He scored 68 goals in the Premier League for Everton and Newcastle United, and has since become a coach at Goodison Park. •

BARTON

ETIHAD STADIUM, MANCHESTER, U.K.

13 MAY 2012

TAKES ON MAN CITY

Joey Barton was involved in his fair share of controversy as a player. The one-time England midfielder certainly appeared to mellow in the latter part of his career, becoming a key member of the Queens Park Rangers and Burnley teams that won promotion to the Premier League in 2014 and 2016 respectively. Before that, red cards, suspensions, and off-field indiscretions clouded his on-field achievements.

Barton's most notable dismissal came while playing for QPR against Manchester City, the club for whom he had made his professional debut. It was the final day of the 2011–12 season, and it was a huge day for both clubs. City could seal a first league title for 44 years with a victory at Etihad Stadium, while QPR were still not safe from relegation.

It was 1-1 early in the second half when the flashpoint came. Barton and City striker, Carlos Tevez, clashed on the edge of the QPR penalty area. Barton claimed Tevez punched him, and retaliated with an elbow to the face that left Argentina international Tevez on the floor. It was spotted by the assistant referee, which led to referee, Mike Dean, dismissing Barton.

Enveloped in red mist, Barton kicked out at Sergio Agüero, who fell to the ground. With tempers flaring on both sides, City captain, Vincent Kompany, got involved, and as he advanced towards Barton, the QPR man sent his head in Kompany's direction. The ramifications for Barton would be severe: a 12-match suspension and a £75,000 fine from the Football Association, while QPR imposed their own sanctions – he was stripped of the captaincy and fined six weeks' wages by the London club.

The midfielder has acknowledged publicly that he made a "wrong decision", but has also said that he felt he was in full control of his emotions. His intention was to try to get a City player sent off as well, so that the numbers would be evened up, which goes a long way to explaining the events that followed after he had seen the red card.

In the game, City enjoyed a remarkable injury-time comeback that clinched them the Premier League title, while QPR stayed up despite their 3-2 loss and Barton's moment of madness. •

"I heard Bobby Zamora hissing, 'take one with you'. We laugh about it now, but I remember thinking 'good idea'."

JOEY BARTON

RED-CARD

**VARIOUS
STADIUMS**

**REPEAT
OFFENCES**

RAMOS

Sergio Ramos has won pretty much everything there is to win in football, both at club level with Real Madrid and on the international stage with Spain. His career has been littered with success: numerous Champions League triumphs, a World Cup win, and two European Championship victories. But it also has its caveats, his less than exemplary disciplinary record for one. By the end of the 2017–18 season, Ramos had been shown 24 red cards in his playing career.

Nineteen of those have come in La Liga, a record for Spain's top division, while five have come in matches against Barcelona. Ramos' first "El Clásico" red card in November 2010 was perhaps the most prime example of the red mist overcoming him.

It didn't help that Real Madrid were about to lose 5-0 to their biggest rivals. Ramos had already been booked when he made a wild hack at the legs of the advancing Lionel Messi, who was on yet another mazy run. If that wasn't enough to warrant a red card, pushing both Carles Puyol and Xavi Hernández in the face certainly was. It was a night to forget.

"I am only missing Roberto Firmino saying he got a cold because a drop of my sweat landed on him."

SERGIO RAMOS

Ramos was back in the headlines after the 2018 Champions League final, won by Real against Liverpool in Kiev. His robust first-half grapple with Liverpool's star man Mohamed Salah resulted in the Egyptian being forced off with a shoulder injury. Salah required surgery, which threatened his participation in the 2018 World Cup. Many Liverpool supporters blamed Ramos for Salah's injury and one person went as far as starting an online petition asking UEFA and FIFA to punish Ramos retrospectively.

Ramos said later that Salah "grabbed his arm first" and, after reports that he had also given Liverpool goalkeeper, Loris Karius, a concussion in a collision, Ramos added: "I am only missing Roberto Firmino saying he got a cold because a drop of my sweat landed on him." •

EVRA

ESTÁDIO DOM AFONSO HENRIQUES, GUIMÃRAES, PORTUGAL

2 NOVEMBER 2017

BOOTS FANS

Football supporters can be a fickle bunch sometimes. A sequence of bad performances will all be forgotten if you score the winning goal in a game against your local rivals. Conversely, it does not matter if you scored in every round of a cup competition if you then miss a glorious chance in the final and go on to lose. All that most right-thinking football fans will ask of their players is to give their all. If you lose, so be it, as long as every ounce of blood, sweat, and tears have gone into those past 90 minutes on the football field.

In isolated cases, however, some supporters never manage to get along with a certain player. Take, for example, when France's former captain, Patrice Evra, joined Marseille in January 2017. Ten months later, before a Europa League group game in Portugal, a group of Marseille fans directed abuse towards the left-back – who was due to be a substitute in the match against Vitória Guimarães – as he warmed up.

> **"No matter what happens, a professional player must maintain self-control despite provocations and insults, no matter how unjustified they may be."**
>
> MARSEILLE CLUB STATEMENT

Evra took exception and reportedly kicked a ball towards the travelling supporters. Several Marseille players wandered over in an attempt to calm the situation down, but matters escalated again and Evra reacted by running over and kicking one of the fans in the head.

Evra was shown a red card before kick-off and was suspended by the French club following their 1-0 defeat. In a statement, Marseille condemned the "unacceptable behaviour" of "a handful of provocateurs who uttered particularly serious hateful attacks" against the player, but added that "as a professional and experienced player, Evra could not respond in such an inappropriate way."

UEFA banned the former Manchester United and Juventus defender from European competition for the remainder of the 2017–18 season and his contract with Marseille was later terminated by mutual consent. For a player who made 81 appearances for his country and had been one of the nation's most successful football exports of his era, it was a fiery and sad end to Evra's career in France. •

BLINK AND YOU'LL MISS THEM: FAST RED CARDS

⟶ Uruguay's José Batista holds the record for the fastest red card in World Cup history. The midfielder lasted just 52 seconds of his country's final group game against Scotland at the 1986 World Cup in Mexico when he was sent off for a clumsy lunge on Gordon Strachan. •

⟶ In 1999, Swansea striker Walter Boyd created headlines when he was dismissed for elbowing an opponent in an English fourth-tier match against Darlington. Play hadn't been restarted after Boyd's introduction as a substitute, so the Jamaican was technically sent off after ZERO seconds! •

⟶ Sheffield United's Keith Gillespie was sent off 12 seconds after coming on as a substitute in a Premier League match against Reading in 2007. Awaiting a throw-in to be taken, Gillespie swung an arm in Reading midfielder Stephen Hunt's direction, a clash deemed worthy of a red card by referee, Mark Halsey. He then pushed Hunt in the face as he left the field. •

⟶ Sometimes red cards can tarnish the biggest games of a player's career. Liam Ridehalgh's two-footed tackle on Ricky Shakes earned him a red card after 48 seconds in the 2018 National League promotion final at Wembley. Thankfully for him, it didn't cost Tranmere victory, with Rovers beating Boreham Wood 2-1 to seal their place back in the English Football League. •

⟶ Perhaps surprisingly, some goalkeepers have also been sent for an early bath. Kevin Pressman's 2000–01 season was only 13 seconds old when he was dismissed for handling the ball outside his penalty area in Sheffield Wednesday's opening second-tier match against Wolves at Molineux. And in 2011, Preston Edwards of Ebbsfleet United lasted only 10 seconds of a Conference South game before he saw red for bringing down a Farnborough player who was clean through on goal. •

TEAMS

With local pride, international glory, league placing,
or big trophies at stake, two sides can quickly
become the fiercest of rivals ...

DUST-UP

**WEMBLEY STADIUM,
LONDON, U.K.**

**10 AUGUST
1974**

AT
WEMBLEY

Forty-three years before Anthony Joshua and Wladimir Klitschko fought for heavyweight titles in boxing at a sold-out Wembley Stadium, the venue played host to a punch-up between two of English football's star names. The Charity Shield is English football's annual season opener, pitting the previous season's champions and FA Cup winners against each other. Yes, there is a trophy at stake and it usually includes two of the main title challengers for the upcoming campaign, but often these matches are uneventful and forgettable.

The 1974 edition was a notable exception, though, mainly as a result of a punch-up that left two of the biggest names in British football facing 11-game suspensions. The match had more sub-plots than you could care to imagine.

Champions Leeds United had surprisingly appointed Brian Clough, previously a huge critic of the club, as successor to Don Revie after he had become England manager. Liverpool were under new management, too. Bill Shankly – the man credited with turning the Reds into a major force during the 1960s – had retired and his assistant Bob Paisley had taken charge, although Shankly led the Liverpool team out onto the field one last time. The two clubs had had their run-ins over the previous decade and that was no surprise given they had both been challenging for the league title for much of that time, but not many expected their rivalry to come to a head so spectacularly on that sunny August day at Wembley.

After 60 minutes, Johnny Giles floored Liverpool forward Kevin Keegan with an off-the-ball right hook. A booking, but nothing more for the Leeds man. As the resulting free-kick was cleared, another flare-up erupted, this time involving an understandably irate Keegan and Leeds captain Billy Bremner. This time the punishment was stronger: both were sent off for their part in the incident.

Keegan and Bremner threw their shirts to the ground in disgust as they made their way off the field and down the Wembley tunnel, but worse punishment was to follow.

The Football Association Disciplinary Committee charged both men with bringing the game into disrepute and the duo, on top of their automatic three-match suspensions, were banned for a further eight games and fined £500 each.

As for the match itself, it ended in a 1-1 draw. Liverpool won 6-5 in a penalty shootout, with Leeds goalkeeper, David Harvey, missing the only spot-kick. •

"They're both throwing their shirts down, and really this is a side of English football we do not want to see."

BBC COMMENTATOR, BARRY DAVIES

THE BATTLE

**BASEBALL GROUND,
DERBY, U.K.**

**1 NOVEMBER
1975**

OF THE
BASEBALL
GROUND

A year after Kevin Keegan and Billy Bremner had traded at blows in the 1974 Charity Shield at Wembley (see page 82), Leeds United were involved in more on-field fisticuffs, this time in a league match against Derby County. The flames of an impending fracas were fanned by a debatable penalty decision given against the Yorkshire club in the first half. Leeds defender Norman Hunter made minimal contact, if any, with Derby striker Francis Lee as he chased the ball but the referee pointed to the spot.

More fireworks were to come. Lee and Hunter collided as the former let fly with the shot from the edge of the penalty box in the second half. The pair squared up and, while play continued on the other side of the field, Hunter landed a punch that dropped Lee to his knees, and split his lip. Other players and the referee quickly stepped in to make sure the bust-up would go no further, after which both Lee and Hunter were sent off.

The situation had been dealt with. Or at least, so everyone thought. As the two made their way towards the tunnel, another fight broke out. Lee's arms were swinging like windmills, trying and failing to connect with Hunter. Another commotion followed, before both were led away by coaching staff. •

"It's broken out again! And now this time, a complete free-for-all."

BBC COMMENTATOR, JOHN MOTSON

WHEN TEAMMATES

**ST JAMES' PARK,
NEWCASTLE, U.K.**

**2 APRIL
2005**

COLLIDE

Football is a team sport. However talented you are, you can't or won't win anything without the help of your teammates. That said, you're not going to get along with everyone you play alongside. Ex-professionals will tell you that arguments on the training field are fairly regular occurrences. But as long as you don't take any disagreements or ill-feeling with you over the white line and onto the field, everything should be fine, shouldn't it? Well, not always.

Newcastle United pair, Kieron Dyer and Lee Bowyer made unwanted headlines when they came to blows during a Premier League match against Aston Villa in 2005. Players from both sides stepped in to separate the two England internationals, who were sent off as a result of the fracas. But what caused two colleagues to want to fight each other?

The Magpies were 3-0 down at home at the time, so that obviously didn't help. In subsequent interviews, Dyer has said Bowyer was angry at him as he wasn't passing him the ball, while Bowyer put the incident down to a "moment of madness." Bowyer let Dyer know in no uncertain terms that he wanted the ball, and Dyer later admitted to telling him where to go, which caused Bowyer to erupt. After the match, both players offered a swift and comprehensive apology. Bowyer was fined six weeks' wages for his part in the on-field bust-up, and received a four-match ban. Dyer was adjudged to have been less to blame, and escaped with just a three-match ban.

This wasn't the first instance of two teammates squaring up on the field. Ten years earlier, Blackburn Rovers duo, Graeme Le Saux and David Batty were involved in a similar incident in a Champions League match in Russia. All was not well in the lead-up, with Le Saux since admitting divisions had started to form between the two before it finally came to a head against Spartak Moscow. Early in the game, the pair both tried to retrieve the ball from near the touchline but collided into each other. That moment of miscommunication and the simmering tensions between the two proved too much for Le Saux and Batty to ignore, with Le Saux breaking his hand as he threw a punch at the midfielder. Although they were not sent off on the night, both players were fined by their club and banned by UEFA. •

"Words between players – hard words between players – occur in every game of football and it is very unusual for it to lead to what happened today."

GRAEME SOUNESS

CAMEROON

**SAN SIRO,
MILAN, ITALY**

**8 JUNE
1990**

CRUSH
CANIGGIA

Every once in a while, there's a team at a major tournament that captures the imagination of supporters across the globe. In 1990, that team was Cameroon. They became the first African nation to reach the quarter-finals of a World Cup, gaining fans and friends along the way before losing in extra-time to England in the last eight. Much of the love for the "Indomitable Lions" came from causing one of the biggest shocks in World Cup history in the very first game of Italia 90.

An unheralded team, who were ranked outsiders to win the World Cup, beat defending champions Argentina 1-0 in Milan despite ending the game with nine men. Cameroon's physical approach thwarted the talents of Diego Maradona, the undoubted superstar of his era, and his Argentina teammates.

Cameroon had already seen André Kana-Biyik sent off before his brother scored an iconic World Cup goal. François Omam-Biyik's tame second-half header somehow escaped the grasp of Argentina goalkeeper Nery Pumpido and trickled into the corner of the net. With the match heading into stoppage time and Cameroon still leading, Argentina striker Claudio Caniggia collected the ball on the edge of his own penalty area and set off in pursuit of an equalising goal that would save the face of his country's football team. Caniggia slipped by one limp attempt at a Cameroon tackle just inside his own half.

On he went. In front of him stood another green-shirted defender, who tried his best to end the counter-attack by foul means, but Caniggia rode a wild challenge. On he went.

Next up was Benjamin Massing. Caniggia, struggling to regain his balance, nudged the ball ahead. Massing was late and reckless, and caught Caniggia with a body check.

The force of the tackle was so much that Massing's boot came off in the process. It wasn't the sort of challenge you want to make when you've already been shown a yellow card, either. Massing was sent off, but Cameroon would not be deterred. Their nine men held out for the remaining few minutes and completed one of international football's biggest upsets. •

"I don't think they had any intentions of beating us up to win the game. I cannot argue, and I cannot make excuses. If Cameroon won, it was because they were the best side."

DIEGO MARADONA

On he went ...

on he went ...

THE BATTLES

**OLD TRAFFORD,
MANCHESTER, U.K.**

**REPEAT
OFFENCES**

OF OLD
TRAFFORD

Manchester United and Arsenal are two of the biggest clubs in English football. Every year, they are there-or-thereabouts in the hunt for trophies, so it is only natural that every so often they do not get along all that well ...

There are several examples of the Red Devils and the Gunners clashing on and off the field, but we shall focus on three incidents here. Firstly, there was the 21-man brawl at Old Trafford in October 1990 that resulted in both teams being docked league points. Arsenal were leading 1-0 with a goal from Anders Limpar when tempers flared. Gunners left-back Nigel Winterburn flew into a challenge on Denis Irwin, causing him and teammate Brian McClair to retaliate by kicking the grounded Winterburn. Every player bar Arsenal goalkeeper David Seaman piled in, many of them attempting to calm the situation down. Only two players were booked, but afterwards United were deducted one point for their role in the incident and Arsenal two, having been involved in a similar fracas during the previous season. The Gunners overcame that points sanction, however, to win the league title.

Thirteen years later, there was another confrontation in a fiery Premier League contest between the teams at Old Trafford.

United looked well placed to win the battle of the two title favourites when, in stoppage time, they were awarded a penalty against 10-man Arsenal. Ruud van Nistelrooy (who had been involved in the incident that saw Gunners midfielder Patrick Vieira dismissed), smacked his spot-kick off the crossbar. With a goalless draw all but confirmed, several Arsenal players ran to Van Nistelrooy to celebrate. Among them was Martin Keown, who jumped in the air and landed his arms hard on the Dutchman's back.

Keown was one of four Arsenal players to be retrospectively suspended, while the club was fined £175,000 as a result of their players' actions. Arsenal's "Invincibles" went on to win the Premier League title without losing a match. It was the first time in more than a century that a team had gone through an English top-division season completely unbeaten.

Their streak without defeat had been extended to an English record of 49 matches when Arsenal returned to Old Trafford in October 2004. It was another ugly game that contained several unsavoury incidents, but ended with something *actually* savoury being thrown in the direction of United boss, Sir Alex Ferguson ...

United's Rio Ferdinand was lucky to stay on the field after a professional foul on Arsenal's Freddie Ljungberg, while Van Nistelrooy escaped a red card for a nasty tackle on Ashley Cole. Arsenal's anger increased when Sol Campbell's outstretched leg invited Wayne Rooney to go down in the penalty area. Campbell withdrew his leg and despite minimal contact between the England teammates, referee, Mike Riley, pointed to the spot and signalled for a penalty kick. Van Nistelrooy converted from 12 yards to give United a precious lead. The two sets of players clashed in the tunnel after United's 2-0 victory, and in the chaos Ferguson was hit by a piece of pizza!

The identity of the pizza-flinger remained a mystery for many years, until Spanish midfielder, Cesc Fàbregas, revealed in 2017 that it was he who was the guilty party. •

"Look at this. This is disgraceful. It's a free-for-all and how will the referee be able to sort it all out?"

ITV COMMENTATOR, MARTIN TYLER

THE
BATTLE

**BRAMALL LANE,
SHEFFIELD, U.K.**

**16 MARCH
2002**

OF
BRAMALL
LANE

The English second-tier match between Sheffield United and West Bromwich Albion in March 2002 was labelled the "Battle of Bramall Lane", and with good reason. The game had to be abandoned with eight minutes remaining as three red cards and two injuries had left the Blades with only six players.

Early on, Sheffield United's goalkeeper, Simon Tracey, was sent off for handling the ball outside his penalty area. But it wasn't until the midway point of the second half, with Albion leading 2-0, that things started to go really awry.

United substitute Georges Santos had been on the field for less than a minute when he lunged into a dangerous tackle on Baggies midfielder, Andy Johnson. The two had history: Santos had been left with a fractured cheekbone in an aerial challenge with Johnson a year earlier. Santos was shown a red card and a huge brawl followed, during which another Blades substitute Patrick Suffo headbutted Albion captain Derek McInnes and was the third Sheffield United player to be sent from the field.

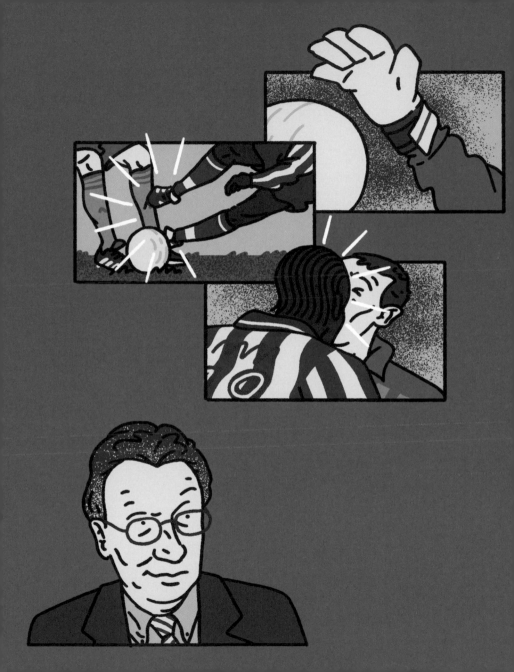

The Baggies extended their lead to 3-0 against the Blades, now down to eight men, but would not complete victory inside 90 minutes. Sheffield United's Michael Brown and Rob Ullathorne, left the pitch with injuries, and referee Eddie Wolstenholme brought the match to an early conclusion. The ref had no choice, as Sheffield United had only six players left on the pitch, one fewer than the regulation seven required for a game to continue.

The result was later allowed to stand by the Football League, helping West Brom secure promotion to England's top flight a month later, while Sheffield United, manager Neil Warnock, player-coach Keith Curle, Santos, and Suffo were all fined. Santos and Suffo were immediately transfer-listed, and never played for the club again. •

"I wouldn't imagine Gary (Megson) will be having a drink with me tonight, no. But then, not many managers do."

NEIL WARNOCK

THE FRENCH

**KNYSNA,
SOUTH AFRICA**

**20 JUNE
2010**

REVOLT

It has almost been all-or-nothing if you have followed France at major tournaments over the past two decades. Either they excel and go all the way to the title, as they did at the 1998 and 2018 World Cups, or they head home early with their tails between their legs, as they did in 2002 and 2010. But, even by their standards, the 2010 World Cup in South Africa represented a new low.

Even their qualification for the tournament was controversial: Thierry Henry was both offside and used his hand to control the ball as he crossed for William Gallas' winning goal in their play-off victory over the Republic of Ireland. Once they got to South Africa, things started to go wrong. A opening draw with Uruguay was followed by a disapointing loss to Mexico, where striker, Nicolas Anelka, was sent home after clashing with French coach, Raymond Domenech, at half-time. The cracks within the team started to appear, and after the game, the French players revolted.

"It's a scandal for the French, for the federation and the French team."

FRENCH FOOTBALL FEDERATION MANAGING DIRECTOR, JEAN-LOUIS VALENTIN

An open training session quickly descended into farce when the squad refused to take part, retreating instead to their team bus in protest at the Anelka decision. The media looked on in disbelief as captain Patrice Evra argued with the squad's fitness coach. Domenech read a prepared statement signed by the team: "All the players without exception want to declare their opposition to the decision taken by the French Football Federation (FFF) to exclude Nicolas Anelka from the squad," it said. Even after that drama, France retained hopes of reaching the last 16. A win over hosts South Africa could have been enough to take them through, but a 2-1 defeat left them heading home in disgrace.

Afterwards, the team was heavily criticised by both the FFF, and even the French government. Seen as the ringleader, Evra was stripped of the captaincy, and was one of five players banned by the FFF. He returned to the team in 2012. •

WEIRD AND AND WONDERFUL: MORE STRANGE BIRDS

⟶ Liverpool defender, Jamie Carragher, was sent off for throwing a coin into the crowd during an FA Cup tie against Arsenal at Highbury in 2002. Dennis Bergkamp's reckless foul on Carragher saw the Arsenal man dismissed, but England international Carragher, soon followed him down the tunnel. He reached down to pick up a coin thrown at him by an Arsenal supporter and returned it forcefully into the stand. •

⟶ Chelsea's League Cup semi-final second leg at Swansea City in 2013 ended early for Belgium attacker Eden Hazard, who clashed with a teenage ballboy at the Liberty Stadium. Hoping to stall play as Swansea led 2-0 in the tie, the ballboy flopped on top of the loose ball as it rolled out of play for a goal kick. As Hazard tried to kick the ball free, the youngster was left clutching his ribs and writhing in pain on the floor. •

⟶ Somerset Sunday league player Lee Todd saw red after only TWO seconds of a match in 2000. Todd, a striker for Cross Farm Park Celtic, reacted to the referee's first whistle by saying "F**k me, that was loud!" and was dismissed for using foul and abusive language. •

⟶ During a World Cup qualifier in 2013, Argentina's Javier Mascherano received a red card for kicking the driver of the medical buggy that was carrying him from the pitch. •

⟶ When a dog interrupted a Argentine lower-league match in 2013 by running onto the field, José Jiménez quite literally took matters into his own hands – by grabbing the animal around the neck and throwing it several feet into a perimeter fence. Thankfully, the dog appeared to be unharmed. Jiménez was sent off and later had his contract terminated by his club as a result of his actions. •

MANAGERS

They are supposed to be a calming influence on their players but, when the pressure is on, even the most composed managers can lose their cool ...

KEEGAN WOULD

**ELLAND ROAD,
LEEDS, U.K.**

**30 APRIL
1996**

"LOVE IT"

Put a football manager in front of a camera after a match and magic happens every once in a while.

Exhibit A: Kevin Keegan in 1996. Keegan's Newcastle were 12 points clear at the top of the Premier League in January and were the bookies' favourites to win the title. However, Manchester United clawed the deficit back, and by the penultimate weekend of the season the two teams were neck-and-neck at the summit.

In stepped United boss, Sir Alex Ferguson, who claimed that teams such as Nottingham Forest (United's opponents that weekend) and Leeds (Newcastle's opposition) would not try as hard against the Magpies as they would against his team. Newcastle still had to play Forest in the league, while the two sides were also due to face each other in Stuart Pearce's testimonial match at the end of the campaign. Ferguson was clearly trying to influence all involved, and stir things up a bit. Keegan wasn't happy.

After a 1-0 win at Leeds, which left Newcastle three points behind leaders United with a game in hand and two matches left to play, he snapped. The following exchange with Sky Sports presenter Richard Keys, televised live, has gone down in English football folklore:

"That sort of stuff, we're bigger than that."

KEVIN KEEGAN

"That's part and parcel of the psychological battle, Kevin, isn't it?"

RICHARD KEYS

"No! When you do that with footballers like he said about Leeds, and when you do things like that about a man like Stuart Pearce ... I've kept really quiet, but I'll tell you something, he went down in my estimations when he said that. We have not resorted to that. You can tell him now if he's watching ... We're still fighting for this title, and he's got to go to Middlesbrough and get something. And I'll tell you, honestly, I will love it if we beat them. LOVE IT!"

KEVIN KEEGAN

It was the perfect illustration of Keegan as a manager: open, expressive, and passionate.

What it also showed was that he was feeling the pressure from Ferguson, who was winning the managerial mind-games and would later pip Keegan to the title. Draws against Forest and Tottenham put paid to Newcastle's hopes, and the Red Devils went on to win a league and cup double. •

"I WILL LOVE IT IF WE BEAT THEM. LOVE IT!"

KEVIN KEEGAN

CLOUGH

CITY GROUND,
NOTTINGHAM, U.K.

**18 JANUARY
1989**

CLEARS
THE PITCH

It is a commonly-held view that Brian Clough is the greatest English manager never to manage England. He won league titles with both Derby County and Nottingham Forest, before leading Forest to European Cup success in two consecutive seasons. He was a football genius, but with that came a remarkable personality that has gone unmatched in the game since – one that made him much loved by most of the British public, but also saw him overstep the mark on occasion.

One such moment was in January 1989, when Forest supporters invaded the pitch following a 5-2 win over Queens Park Rangers in a League Cup tie at the City Ground.

Violence at football matches was, sadly, a common occurrence in the 80s, but for the most part it appears the encroachment on that night was celebratory rather than to incite trouble.

Clough wanted to clear the pitch as quickly as possible, but did so by punching several fans as the two sets of players made their way down the tunnel.

There was widespread condemnation of Clough's actions. One of the supporters said in a television news interview: "I thought it was a Queens Park Rangers fan who had hit me. I turned round and I just couldn't believe it: it was Brian Clough. He's shouting 'get off the pitch' to everyone and swinging his fists all over."

Clough was fined £5,000 and banned from the touchline for the remainder of the season.

A couple of days after the incident, Clough met with two of the fans that he had punched in a press conference and apologised. It all ended in typical Clough fashion, with the two supporters planting a kiss on his cheek. •

"He was just swinging around like a madman, he was. He was hitting people at random."

NOTTINGHAM FOREST SUPPORTER, SEAN O'HARA

THE
BOOT

**OLD TRAFFORD,
MANCHESTER, U.K.**

**15 FEBRUARY
2003**

AND
BECKHAM

Not many players crossed Sir Alex Ferguson and came out on top. Big stars such as Roy Keane and Jaap Stam had their say on perceived issues at the club and felt the full force of Ferguson's anger as a result.

This time it was David Beckham who found himself on the wrong end of Ferguson's fabled verbal "hairdryer" treatment. After an FA Cup fifth-round loss to Arsenal, Sir Alex felt that Beckham had not done enough for the team to prevent Arsenal's second goal ...

"On European nights, he would come out onto the pitch, start taking penalties and free-kicks and tell us how great he was when he played. The time I really got to find out how great he was came against Arsenal. I'd made a couple of mistakes, he started to walk over to me in the changing room and kicked a pile of clothes on the floor. Out came this boot, it hit me, and then I realised how accurate he was."

DAVID BECKHAM

As Ferguson tore strips of Beckham, he kicked a pile of clothes lying on the floor. Concealed inside was a loose boot which struck the England captain in the face. Beckham sustained a cut above his eye, and later emerged with a plaster over the wound in full view. The story ran for a few weeks, with the famous image of Beckham's plaster – compounded by his hair being fixed back, away from the graze, by a hairband – repeatedly shown on the news and on the sports pages of newspapers.

That was the moment, Ferguson said in his 2013 autobiography, he decided that Beckham would need to be sold. Beckham, he felt, had become too famous and too media-savvy, and Ferguson saw his profile and authority at the club in danger of being eclipsed by his midfield maestro.

United went on to win the Premier League title in the 2002–03 season, which would turn out to be Beckham's last in England. In the summer of 2003, he joined Spanish giants Real Madrid. •

PARDEW'S

KCOM STADIUM,
HULL, U.K.

1 MARCH
2014

HEADBUTT

It's not just the players who can lose their cool. Managers can be just as culpable when the pressure is on or when the moment conspires. Alan Pardew fell foul of both his club and the FA in spectacular fashion while in charge of Newcastle United in 2014. The Magpies' 4-1 Premier League win at Hull City was overshadowed by Pardew's clash with Tigers midfielder, David Meyler. Meyler was attempting to retrieve the ball after it had gone out of play, but Pardew stood in his way. The Hull midfielder pushed Pardew to one side, leading the Newcastle manager to square up to Meyler. In the ensuing conflict, the two came together and Pardew shoved his head towards the Republic of Ireland international midfielder.

Referee, Kevin Friend, booked Meyler and sent Pardew to the stands. Pardew's apology was swift: he said it would be a "wake-up call" that would lead him to remain seated from the dugout from then on. Newcastle fined him £100,000, before the Football Association added an additional £60,000 fine and banned him for seven matches: the longest suspension ever imposed on a Premier League manager.

"I've been involved in a couple of incidents on the line, probably because I'm too near the action. I'll be sitting down from now on and quite rightly after that. I apologise to everyone. I shouldn't have got involved."

ALAN PARDEW

SOUNESS

**SÜKRÜ SARACOGLU STADIUM,
ISTANBUL, TURKEY**

**24 APRIL
1996**

PLANTS
GALATASARAY
FLAG

Every fan will have their own opinion on which teams can claim the title of "the fiercest rivalry in football". Galatasaray and Fenerbahçe will surely argue it is theirs, typified by one incident at the end of their 1996 Turkish Cup final.

Galatasaray's manager during that season was Scotland's Graeme Souness. He was a tough-tackling midfielder; never shy of being combative and competitive on the pitch. In fact, he could have made the list of red mist moments for a couple of incidents he was involved with during his playing career! And, as a manager, he could be just as fiery.

Galatasaray won the home leg of the final 1-0 with a goal from Welsh striker, Dean Saunders, meaning a draw in the return leg would be enough to secure the trophy.

"I managed to get out of there relatively scot-free. Relatively."

GRAEME SOUNESS

Fenerbahçe – who would shortly afterwards be confirmed as league champions – took the lead in the second leg to even the tie, but Saunders popped up again with a thunderous shot into the top corner that earned a 2-1 aggregate win for Galatasaray. The celebrations – as you might expect when you beat your local rivals in a big cup final – ran wild. But Souness took them to the next level.

He was handed a large flag in the red and yellow of Galatasaray and waved it vigorously to gee up the away fans, before racing back onto the pitch and planting it in the centre circle. By literally and metaphorically sinking a flag into enemy territory, Souness committed a most provocative act. It's surprising he managed to get out alive!

Twenty years on, Souness explained his actions. He had done it to prove a point to a Fenerbahçe vice-president, who had asked what Galatasaray were doing "signing a cripple". Souness had had heart surgery a couple of years previously. He added: "When I planted it and turned around, I quickly realised there were a number of [Fenerbahçe] supporters trying to get on to the pitch. I managed to get out of there relatively scot-free. Relatively."

WENGER VS. MOURINHO:

THE BEST OF
ENEMIES

There was a beautiful end to one of the Premier League's fiercest managerial rivalries when, in April 2018, José Mourinho's Manchester United faced Arsene Wenger's Arsenal at Old Trafford for the last time. Wenger had announced he would be stepping down as Arsenal boss at the end of the season after 22 years in the role. Before his final visit to Old Trafford, Mourinho and another of Wenger's great rivals, Sir Alex Ferguson, made a special presentation to the Frenchman as a celebration of his achievements.

It is fair to say, however, that they had not always got on.

If Wenger changed the face of English football when he joined Arsenal in 1996, Mourinho's proclamation that he was the "Special One" when he became Chelsea boss in 2004 took it into a whole new era. Suddenly, managers of top clubs were becoming the stars themselves, sometimes even more so than the players.

"If he respects me even 50 per cent of what I respect him, we can even be friends in the future. I have lots of respect for him. But the reality is that he was at Arsenal, he was the champion, and I came to the country in 2004 and wanted to steal his title. That's football."

JOSÉ MOURINHO

Ferguson, Wenger, Mourinho and Liverpool's Rafael Benítez, all had their various clashes during their reigns of England's leading clubs. Mourinho and Wenger were consistently involved in wars of words, even after Mourinho had left the Premier League to take charge of Inter Milan and then Real Madrid.

It escalated further upon Mourinho's return to Stamford Bridge. In 2014, Wenger claimed that Premier League managers were playing down their club's title chances because they "fear to fail". Mourinho responded by saying Wenger – who at that stage had gone almost nine years without lifting a major trophy – was a "specialist in failure".

In October 2014, the pair were involved in some pushing and shoving on the touchline as tensions boiled over during another tetchy contest between their respective clubs.

Wenger took exception to Gary Cahill's challenge on Alexis Sánchez and marched into the Chelsea technical area, which led to a heated confrontation between the two managers.

Though their rivalry had its fair share of red mist moments over the years, this is one that seems to have ended amicably when Wenger relinquished his role with Arsenal in 2018. •

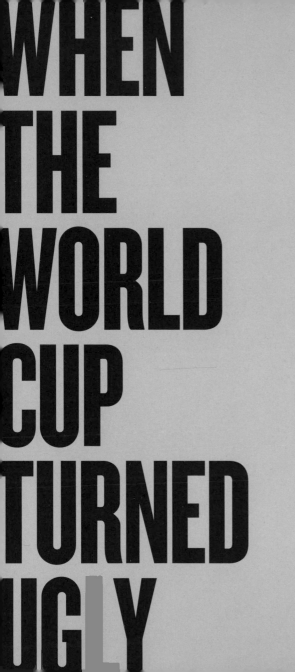

WHEN
THE
WORLD
CUP
TURNED
UGLY

⟶ The group match between World Cup hosts, Chile and Italy in 1962 was labelled the "Battle of Santiago". Two Italy players were sent off, police were called to intervene several times and BBC commentator, David Coleman, described it as "the most stupid, appalling, disgusting, and disgraceful exhibition of football, possibly in the history of the game." The referee, Ken Aston, would later invent yellow and red cards, perhaps inspired by the battle! •

⟶ A World Cup final record 14 cards were shown in the 2010 match between Spain and the Netherlands. Twelve players received yellow cards, while Dutch centre-back John Heitinga was sent off for two bookable offences by English referee Howard Webb. •

⟶ Sixteen cards were shown in the last-16 tie between Portugal and Netherlands at the 2006 World Cup. Four players were sent off, with both sides ending the match with nine men. There were slightly fewer goals than bookings – Portugal won 1-0 to progress to the quarter-finals. •

⟶ Five players have been sent off in World Cup finals: Argentina duo Pedro Monzón and Gustavo Dezotti (1990), France pair Marcel Desailly (1998) and Zinedine Zidane (2006) and Netherlands defender John Heitinga (2010). •

⟶ Turkey's Hakan Ünsal's red card during a World Cup match against Brazil in 2002 was particularly ugly, but not because of him. Annoyed by Brazilian time-wasting, Ünsal kicked the ball at Brazil's Rivaldo with the ball out of play. The ball struck Rivaldo's leg, but he went down clutching his face, pretending to have been seriously injured. Ünsal was sent off, but Rivaldo's appalling behaviour saw him fined and heavily criticised for his play-acting. •

HOW DID THEY GET AWAY WITH THAT?

Football fans have learned to expect the unexpected over the years. Following are the extraordinary moments – the good, the bad and the bizarre – that happen all the time in the crazy world of football.

THE
BIG
BAD
WOLFIE

**ASHTON GATE,
BRISTOL, U.K.**

**7 NOVEMBER
1998**

THE
THREE
LITTLE
PIGS

A big bad wolf once blew down houses made of straw and sticks before being flummoxed by a house made of bricks, so the famous fable goes. This oldest and fiercest of rivalries was renewed at Ashton Gate in 1998.

Bristol City hosted Wolves in an English second-tier match, but Wanderers' thumping 6-1 victory mattered little in the aftermath.

Local and national television news bulletins had their "and finally ..." item sorted with details of a half-time spat between a bunch of men wearing big furry costumes. Wolfie of Wolves clashed with three little pigs who were promoting a double-glazing company. It isn't quite known what turned a penalty shootout between the quartet nasty, but not by the hair on their chinny-chin-chins was this going to pass without incident.

Punches were thrown. Yes, really. Bristol City's mascot, City Cat, became an unlikely peacemaker. You couldn't make it up! •

"I always had my own fans in mind. I was defending the honour of our club."

WOLFIE, AKA STEVE BIRD

DIEGO MARADONA'S

**ESTADIO AZTECA,
MEXICO CITY, MEXICO**

**22 JUNE
1986**

HAND OF GOD

He is one of the best players ever to kick a football around, but controversy was never too far from Diego Armando Maradona. Maradona played in four World Cups, carrying the weight of a football-mad nation on his shoulders for more than a decade, and it is the 1986 tournament in Mexico that will be remembered as "Maradona's World Cup".

His role in Argentina's quarter-final win over England could arguably sum up his whole career: his "Hand of God" goal riled the football world, but it was followed by a moment of genius that left that same football world marvelling at his brilliance.

Early in the second half, Maradona attempted to play a one-two with a teammate. A botched clearance by England's Steve Hodge looped the ball high in the air, and, as it came down into the penalty area, Maradona went up to challenge England's goalkeeper, Peter Shilton.

"I was waiting for my teammates to embrace me and no
one came. I told them 'come
hug me or the referee isn't
going to allow it'."

DIEGO MARADONA

Nobody could quite believe that a midfielder standing at 5 ft 5 in (1.65 m) tall could get above a goalkeeper to head the opening goal.
That's because he didn't.

The television replays told the real story of Maradona's goal. As he said afterwards, the goal had been scored "a little with the head of Maradona and a little with the hand of God".

The moment of brilliance came four minutes later. Maradona picked the ball up inside his own half, turned away from Peter Beardsley and Peter Reid, and proceeded to glide through the England defensive line before rounding Shilton to slide the ball into the net.

BBC commentator Barry Davies said simply: "Oh, you have to say that's magnificent. There is no debate about that goal. That was just pure football genius." It was voted as FIFA's Goal of the Century and it helped Argentina on their way to the last four. Two more Maradona goals in the semi-final against Belgium secured a spot in the final, in which Argentina beat West Germany 3-2 to win the World Cup for the second time.

THE HAMMERS'

**LONDON STADIUM,
LONDON, U.K.**

**10 MARCH
2018**

HAMMER

West Ham United was not a happy football club towards the end of the 2017–18 season.

The team was struggling on the field, there was resentment from the club's move from Upton Park to the London Stadium, as well as a perceived lack of investment in the transfer market. At a Premier League game against Burnley in March 2018, some supporters made their feelings clear.

When the Hammers fell behind in the second half, a fan ran onto the field towards captain Mark Noble, who wrestled the invader to the ground and forcefully asked him to leave the pitch in no uncertain terms.

In another of several pitch encroachments, one person picked up one of the corner flags and planted it in the centre circle. A large group of West Ham supporters vented their fury towards the directors' box and co-owners David Sullivan and David Gold were advised to leave their seats and head inside the stadium because of fears for their safety. It was an ugly afternoon.

"I'm a West Ham fan and I've always protected the club," Noble told BBC Sport after the match. "If someone approaches me, I'll protect myself. Every time we lose we and the board get a lot of stick. It seemed today that the fans had had enough."

West Ham gave several supporters life bans following the pitch invasions and the club was charged by the Football Association. •

"Every time we lose we and the board get a lot of stick. It seemed today that the fans had had enough."

MARK NOBLE

A DIFFERENT KIND OF

PLOUGH LANE, LONDON, U.K.

6 FEBRUARY 1988

BALL GAME

A shirt pull here, a tread on the toes there: as long as it doesn't get seen by the officials, some players will resort to almost anything to gain an upper hand over their opponents.

Lots tried, and often failed, to stop Paul Gascoigne (Gazza) dominating matches before and after his exploits with England at the 1990 World Cup. Vinnie Jones attempted something a little bit different to seize an advantage.

Gazza was the brightest young talent in English football in February 1988. Tottenham were soon to spend more than £2 million to sign the Newcastle United midfielder, and he was just about to break into the full England squad for the first time. Jones – one of the game's hard men – was given the task of trying to mark Gazza, and did so brilliantly, helping his Wimbledon side to a goalless draw in their First Division match at Plough Lane.

In what became one of football's iconic photographs, Jones was seen reaching behind him to grab Gascoigne's testicles, leaving Gascoigne squealing in pain. It is both hilarious and terrifying – Jones' rough tactics offset by Gazza's mock (or is it real?) pain.

In a 2015 documentary profiling his career, Gascoigne says he sent a red rose to Jones after the incident. Jones responded by sending Gascoigne a toilet brush, and they have been good friends ever since. •

"I was coming out of the tunnel. He looked at me and said 'it's me and you, fat boy'. He followed me everywhere."

PAUL GASCOIGNE

A HISTORY OF ENGLAND'S RED CARDS

⟶ Up to the end of the 2018 World Cup, England players had been on the receiving end of 15 red cards...

⟶ England have playing international football for more than a century, but four of those 15 red cards came in the space of 15 months between June 1998 and September 1999. David Beckham, Paul Ince, Paul Scholes, and David Batty were the quartet given their marching orders. •

⟶ Alan Mullery was the first man to be sent off playing for England. His dismissal, for kicking Dobrivoje Trivić in retaliation, came in England's semi-final defeat by Yugoslavia at the 1968 European Championships. •

⟶ Robert Green is the only goalkeeper to see red in an England shirt. He was dismissed for bringing down Artem Milevskiy when the Ukrainian attacker was clean through on goal in a World Cup qualifier in 2009. •

⟶ Wayne Rooney is the last England player to be sent off in a major tournament. Rooney clashed with Portugal defender Ricardo Carvalho during England's 2006 World Cup quarter-final loss and was shown a red card after treading on Carvalho's groin. •

⟶ Rooney and Beckham are the only two players to have been sent off twice while playing for England. As well as his red card against Argentina in 1998, Beckham was dismissed for two bookable offences in a World Cup qualifier against Austria in 2005. Rooney's other dismissal was for kicking out at Montenegro's Miodrag Džudović during a European Championship qualifier in 2011. •

"IT WASN'T ME, REF!"

RED CARD BLUNDERS

Everyone makes mistakes, but if you're involved in football they are magnified to a whole new level.

——> Croatia defender, Josip Simunic, received a red card during his country's World Cup group match against Australia in 2006. English referee, Graham Poll, had already booked Simunic but failed to send the centre-back off when he committed a second bookable offence in the game. It was only at the final whistle, when Simunic was booked for a THIRD time for dissent, that a red card was shown. Poll never refereed at international level again. •

——> A bad day at Stamford Bridge got significantly worse for Arsenal, and in particular Kieran Gibbs, when the Gunners lost 6-0 to Chelsea in a Premier League fixture in March 2014. Arsenal were already 2-0 down when Eden Hazard shot towards the net and Alex Oxlade-Chamberlain handled the Chelsea forward's effort on the goal line. Referee, Andre Marriner, awarded Chelsea a penalty and then, surprisingly, sent off Gibbs! The England international left-back rightly had his red card rescinded a few days later. •

——> It's not just the referees who can make red card blunders. Pundit, Chris Kamara, was reporting live on a Premier League between his former club, Portsmouth, and Blackburn Rovers for Sky Sports in 2010, and failed to notice that Portsmouth's, Anthony Vanden Borre, had been sent off. "Have you not been watching?" asked presenter, Jeff Stelling, in the studio. "I don't know Jeff ... the rain must have got in my eyes ... I saw him go off but I thought they were bringing a sub on," replied Kamara. Unbelievable, Jeff! •

4

→ Sanchez Watt was in action for English non-league club, Hemel Hempstead Town, in March 2018 when referee, Dean Hulme, wanted to caution him and asked for his name: "Watt," Watt replied. But Hulme mistook it as "what?" and when the back-and-forth discussion continued in the same fashion, Hulme thought the former Arsenal player was showing dissent and sent him off! When it was explained that "Watt" was indeed his name, the error was quickly rectified and Watt's punishment was reduced to just a yellow card. "I think everybody found it amusing afterwards, including the referee," Hemel Hempstead chairman, Dave Boggins, told BBC Sport. "He was very apologetic and saw the funny side of it." •

5

→ One of the great injustices of France's World Cup victory in 1998 was that defender, Laurent Blanc, was suspended for the final. Blanc had been one of the stars of the host nation's run in the tournament, but he was harshly dismissed in the semi-final win over Croatia following Slaven Bilic's overreaction to a confrontation in the penalty area. As Blanc attempted to push Bilic away in the chest, Bilic collapsed to the ground holding his face. Before matches at that World Cup, Blanc would kiss the bald head of goalkeeper, Fabien Barthez, for good fortune. That job passed to his replacement Frank Leboeuf before the final, and Leboeuf's lips proved just as lucky as those of his suspended team-mate, with France beating Brazil 3-0 in Paris to win the trophy for the first time. •

→ PHIL CARTWRIGHT

Phil Cartwright is a BBC Sport journalist with a huge passion for games involving a ball and some other games that don't.

He has been working for the BBC since 2006, starting out as a local radio presenter and football commentator, before transferring to a position writing for the BBC Sport website.

His highlights include working on a Championship play-off final at Wembley, several World Darts Championships and two Rugby League World Cups. He also shook hands with David Beckham at a Sports Personality of the Year awards ceremony.

This is his first published work.

Outside work, most of his time is spent with two of the loves of his life: his girlfriend, Fran, and his football team, Wolverhampton Wanderers.

Follow Phil on Twitter, @cartosport

→ CHESTER HOLME

Chester Holme is a freelance illustrator from South London. Since graduating from Kingston University in 2015, he has worked for an international array of clients including Nike, Red Bull and OMA. His work is informed by printmaking processes; using flat, bold colours and simple lines and shapes to build image and pattern through layers. As a QPR and England supporter, there haven't been many moments of beauty in Chester's footballing life — instead his interest in the game lies in its ugly, dirty, human side.

→ NOTONSUNDAY

Founded by Mike Willows and Wayne Trevor Townsend, NotOnSunday is an independent London-based brand and design studio. From re-branding the Scouts UK to launching the World Gallery at the Horniman Museum and Gardens their work is extremely varied.

Over the years they've created a number of self initiated football projects that led them to working with Hardie Grant.

This is now their 5th book with commissioning editor, Kajal Mistry, having pitched the *Red Mist* concept in March 2018.

RED MIST
FOOTBALL'S MOST SHOCKING MOMENTS

Published in 2019 by Hardie Grant Books, an imprint of
Hardie Grant Publishing

Hardie Grant Books (London)
5th & 6th Floors
52–54 Southwark Street
London SE1 1UN

Hardie Grant Books (Melbourne)
Building 1, 658 Church Street
Richmond, Victoria 3121

hardiegrantbooks.com

British Library Cataloguing-in-Publication Data.
A catalogue record for this book is available from the British Library.

Red Mist: Football's Most Shocking Moments by Phil Cartwright
ISBN: 978-1-78488-244-0

Publishing Director: Kate Pollard
Commissioning Editor: Kajal Mistry
Copy Editor: Steven Carton
Design and Art Direction: NotOnSunday
Illustrator: Chester Holme

Pages 10–13: reference www.fifa.com/development/education-and-
technical/referees/laws-of-the-game.html

Colour Reproduction by p2d
Printed and bound in China by Leo Paper Group